Heart to Hands Bead Embroidery

Fresh Ideas
and Techniques
for Creating Art
with Beads

Robin Atkins

Heart to Hand Bead Embroidery

Fresh Ideas and Techniques for Creating Art with Beads

Robin Atkins

Copyright © March, 2008

www.robinatkins.com

All rights reserved. No part of this book may be reproduced or transmitted in any form or by any means, electronic or mechanical, including photocopying, without permission in writing from the author. You may contact the author through her website.

ISBN: 978-0-9705538-9-8

Tiger Press
837 Miller Road
Friday Harbor WA 98250

This book is dedicated to the beautiful, innocent and creative inner child who loves playing with beads and making art! My intent is to free the precious voice that originates in our hearts to sing in an ever bolder way.

R. Atkins, 2005

Decade Doll #6

4.5" x 4"; this doll represents my life story from ages 51 through 60.

Contents

Getting started

Introduction 6
Materials 7
Get ready to bead . . . 9

Inspirations

Beaded stories
 & memories 11
Working in series 13
Visual journaling 15
Telling your life
 story 18
Self-portrait 23
Passions 24
People you love 26
Places you love 28
Things you love 32
Causes & concerns . . 32
Personal issues 36
Tributes
 & memorials 42

Techniques

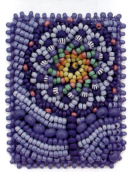

Variations on stacks

    Tall & short stacks .. 48

    Barnacles 50

    Bezels 52

    Half shells 54

    Spiral shells 55

    Ruffles 57

    Flat flowers 59

    Pinwheel flowers . . . 60

    Raised flowers 62

    Wildflowers 63

Surface bumps

    Running water 65

    Petals 66

    Tree trunks 67

Surface fringe

    Loops 68

    Twisted fringe 69

    Twisted lines 71

    Smoke 72

    Branch fringe 73

    Tree branches 75

    Roots 77

Introduction

Pick up a bead you love and start anywhere.
All starting points are equally valid.

Look through these pages and find something compelling. Begin there. Get out a piece of fabric you love, baste it onto a piece of paper or other stabilizer and start beading!

The first part of this book is all about inspirations and ideas for using your everyday experiences to create bead embroidery that is unique and appealing. Perhaps, as you skim these pages, a picture or phrase will grab your attention, trigger a memory or spark a passion. If so, begin right there. Starting with what you already know about bead embroidery, take what you need of the inspirational concept, pick out some beads you love and get to work.

If one of the techniques in the second part of this book catches your eye, try it right away. Practice the stitch a couple of times, try it with different sizes of beads, play with the spacing. In the process, you'll begin to get comfortable with the technique and start to own it.

The focus of this book is aimed toward those who already have some familiarity with bead embroidery. If you have no previous experience, you may wish to begin by learning the four essential stitches (seed stitch, lazy stitch, back stitch and couching). My first bead embroidery book, *One Bead at a Time*, will get you started on the basics.

R. Atkins, 2008

Examples of accents used in bead embroidery include
glass beads in various shapes, buttons, pearls, ceramic animals and many other possibilities.

Materials

Fall in love with your beads.
Have more than enough colors and sizes.

Beads. For most of my bead embroidery and the technique samples in this book, I use only five sizes of seed beads: 5s (the largest), 6s, 8s, 11s and my beloved 15s (the smallest). I also use short bugle beads in most of my work. The picture below is actual size.

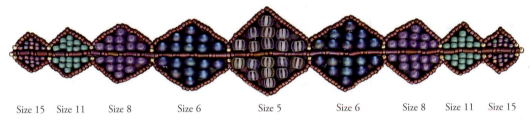

| Size 15 | Size 11 | Size 8 | Size 6 | Size 5 | Size 6 | Size 8 | Size 11 | Size 15 |

A small assortment of glass accent beads, crystals, pearls, stones, small ceramic or bone beads and a cabochon may be fun to incorporate into your designs as well (picture, page 6).

Needles. Although any type of beading needle may be used, I've found short, stiff beading needles manufactured by John James to be the most useful. A size 11 needle will work for most contemporary seed beads. But for the smaller, vintage seed beads, a size 12 needle may be needed. If the bead holes are extra small, use smaller-sized needles (13, 14 or 16).

Thread. There are currently several manufacturers of beading thread suitable for bead embroidery, including Nymo (use size D), Silamide and Superlon (use size AA). My long-time favorite of these is Nymo. It is not desirable to double the thread; use a single strand.

Stabilizer. For beading on cloth, some sort of stabilizer is needed to keep the work from puckering. Older beading books recommend using a hoop for this purpose. However, I find that the hoop will stretch the cloth, causing puckering as it "relaxes" after being removed from the hoop. To stabilize my work, I use computer-weight, acid-free paper. Some art supply and archival shops carry acid-free interleaving paper, which was developed for archival storage of textiles. This is fabulous paper to use if you can find it. Other popular choices include various interfacing materials, Timtex™ and Lacy's Stiff Stuff™.

Fabric. Any and all fabrics will work for bead embroidery. I tend to use printed, quilting-weight cotton or silk. If you are a beginner, you may find stretchy fabrics or fabric with a nap (such as velveteen) quite "character building." Once you're practiced, anything goes.

Tool kit. In your bead embroidery tool kit, you'll find the following items handy to have on hand: a small pair of sharp scissors, a bead scoop or small spoon, a beading cloth for spreading out your beads, a thimble and a pair of chain-nosed pliers. Most of this time, I use a small "project box" to hold the beads for each project, the fabric basted to a piece of stabilizer, my beading cloth, needles and tool kit.

R. Atkins, 2008

Ferns and Flowers

2.5" x 2.25", piece in progress
My working setup includes a bead project box, beading cloth, scissors, bead scoop (souvenir spoon), beads, thread, needle and fabric basted to paper ready to bead.
(The project box shown above contains enough beads for several projects.)

Get Ready to Bead!

Find a haven where you can work comfortably.
Use beads and supplies you already have available.

Choose a small piece of fabric that you love. It doesn't have to be new. Beading on cloth that was once a prom dress, a baby quilt, a well-worn necktie, or other previously used item can be fulfilling in many ways. Cut out a rectangle or square from this fabric. A good size for a beginner is about five or six inches square.

Cut out a piece of stabilizer (page 7) the same size as the fabric. Draw a smaller square or rectangle on the stabilizer, leaving an outside margin of about three quarters of an inch on all sides. Place the stabilizer on your hand, drawing side down. Place the fabric on top of the stabilizer, right side up. Pin them together.

Select a color of beading thread that shows on the fabric, and baste (with a single strand) a line of running stitches following the line drawn on the stabilizer. On the fabric side, you'll now see a basted guideline for your bead embroidery. Sew beads inside the basted square or rectangle. You may sew beads right next to or on the guideline, but not over it.

Choose a thread color for beading. It doesn't have to match the fabric or beads. In fact, I enjoy using a contrasting thread color. Before threading my needle, I stretch the thread to straighten it. This helps to prevent tangling. For bead embroidery, use a single strand of thread about 24 to 30 inches long.

That's it! You are ready to start beading.

Tips

Beading Surfaces. All of the techniques in this book also work for bead embroidery on surfaces other than fabric, such as Ultrasuede™, Timtex™, Lacy's Stiff Stuff™, pellon interfacing, felt, leather or paper.

Altering bead color. You can slightly alter the color of transparent beads with colored thread. For example, if you want the effect of lime green beads, sew transparent yellow beads with green thread.

Thread Color. If you don't want to see the thread, it's generally a good idea to match the fabric rather than the beads.

Eye strain. Shiny-finish, silver-lined and faceted seed beads can be difficult to see, especially when sewing them on a dark fabric. Matte-finish beads and light-colored fabrics are easier on the eyes.

Plain beading surfaces. If you choose to bead on a plain surface (such as pellon interfacing), you can color your design on the surface with fabric paint, marking pens or colored pencils. This will serve two purposes—as a beading guide and as camouflage for small, open spaces between the beads.

Marking designs. To transfer major design elements to your beading fabric, first draw the elements on the under-side of the stabilizer. Then, using a thread color that contrasts with the color of the beading surface, baste a line of running stitches along the drawn lines. You could draw design elements directly on the beading surface. However, since it's difficult to "erase" on fabric, I generally draw on the stabilizer, where I can make corrections, and then baste the guidelines.

Wax. I don't use wax or thread conditioners, because the wax can get on the fabric and beads, becoming a "dirt magnet." A hundred years ago, when the only available threads were made of natural fibers such as cotton, linen or silk, the moisture in the air would eventually cause the thread to rot. Wax was used as a coating on thread to slow the deterioration. Today's threads, made from synthetic materials such as nylon, do not rot and thus do not require treatment.

Knotting off. When your beading thread gets short or you need to move to a different section of your piece, you'll need to make a knot on the wrong side. To make a knot, take a very small stitch very close to where you last sewed to the wrong side. When using paper stabilizer, be sure to catch the fabric in addition to the paper with this stitch. Pull the thread until there is a just a small loop showing. Sew through the loop twice. Slowly pull the thread snug until the loop disappears. Sew under nearby stitches for a distance of about one-half inch. Snip the thread.

Beaded Stories and Memories

*Everyone has stories to tell,
especially when encouraged.*

Toward the end of a memorial service for a very dear friend, her son asked us all to turn to someone nearby and tell a story, such as how we met her or some way that she influenced our lives. Immediately the room came alive with energy and filled with the sounds of memories being shared. I tapped the shoulder of the woman sitting in front of me. She turned with a rapt expression on her face, eager to hear my story and to tell hers. All of us were sharing something personal of ourselves and we didn't want to stop.

This isn't just about memorial services. Every day we crave the opportunity to tell someone about something that happened to us. Did you know you can easily get acquainted with a stranger by asking her/him to tell you a story? It's an irresistible offer, even to a very shy person. That's what I'm asking you to do. Tell your story, share your memories, with beads.

You'll see. The world will want to listen and understand. More than that, you will listen to yourself and perhaps understand yourself better when you use your artwork, whatever type it is, to tell a true story from your own memory and experience.

R. Atkins, 2005

Decade Doll #4

5" x 4.5"
This doll tells the story
of a decade in my life when
I enjoyed many camping,
backpacking and hiking trips
in the mountains of
Washington state.

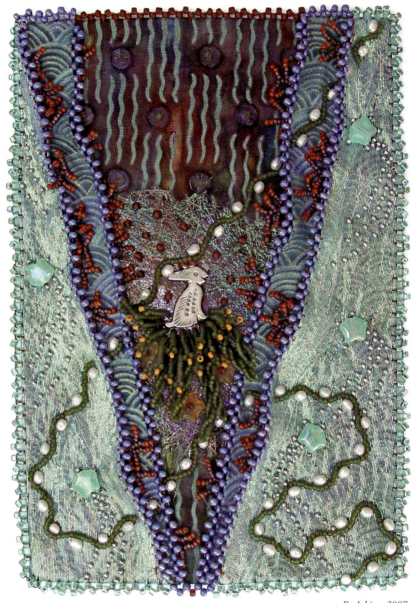

R. Atkins, 2007

Layers

6" x 4", Bead Journal Project, July, #2 in a series of 12 pieces

Working in Series

*Developing your visual voice,
your own unique bead embroidery fingerprint,
is a significant step in becoming an artist.*

One good way to develop your bead embroidery skills and style is to work in series, creating several pieces with one or more things in common. For example, you can make them all the same size, all the same theme or subject, all the same color or all the same technique.

From my own experience, I can tell you that each time I work in series, it becomes a new milestone in my development as an artist. Looking at the work of other artists who make a series of pieces, I see the same thing—rapid growth in confidence, design complexity, skill level and artistic expression. Part of this phenomenon may be explained by the old adage "practice makes perfect." However, I believe that working in series, making several pieces one after another with some elements in common, increases the depth of expression and speeds the journey to excellence faster than making the same number of unrelated pieces.

In addition, I believe working in series promotes a deep spiritual relationship between artist and art, one that can be life-changing, healing and extremely satisfying. By creating many variations on a theme, we can move beyond the mundane and trite to a place where we can explore and embrace the depth of a subject and the process of creation itself. Beyond that, there is a place where we can find peace and self-acceptance.

In the Bead Journal Project (described on page 15), each participant is free to decide what they want to do with their 12 pieces at the end of the year. Some will find a way to bind their work into a book-like journal. Others may frame or mount their pieces. To some, the work is very personal and not intended for sharing. Others will want to show their work.

However, what happens to the work at the end of the year is not so very important. The significant thing is the experience, the process of doing it month after month. With each piece, we become more confident. With each piece, we learn more about how to express our beliefs, concerns and experiences in life. With each piece, our technical skills increase. With each piece, our visual voice becomes stronger and more unique.

R. Atkins, 2007

The Last Leaf

6" x 4", Bead Journal Project, November, #6 in a series of 12 pieces

Visual Journaling

To make art is to give a visual voice to your truth.

In April, 2007 I started the Bead Journal Project, open to anyone who wanted to make a commitment to create one beaded, visual journal piece per month for a year. Soon, with no more than a mention on my blog and website, there were 242 women and one man eager to start. The rules were simple:

1. Beginning in June, 2007, create one piece per month for a year.
2. Every piece must include some beads.
3. You may choose the shape and how large the piece will be, but all 12 pieces must be the same size/shape.

The idea is to give an impression about each month, to journal our experiences and record our feelings in a visual way. Each month, I ask myself, "What is important to me right now and how can I express it?"

Some of the participants create literal representations of their life during the month. For example, one could bead a beach scene with boogie board, towel, umbrella, waves, sand and sun to represent a vacation at the ocean in July. My piece for November, "The Last Leaf," is an example of how one might realistically "tell" about this month of fallen leaves, rain and the first snowstorms of winter (page 14).

Some create work that tells a story with symbols. An example is my piece for October (page 17), which represents a need for change in the way I view my body, a move toward greater respect for it. The feather is both literal (I found it on the second day of a new daily walking program) and symbolic (flying away from my old habits and negative body image).

Others do work that is entirely abstract, creating a mood of color, form and texture that represents an experience without direct clues for the viewer as to the meaning of the piece.

All of these are valid ways to tell our personal stories.

Try This

Does visual journaling appeal to you? Why not jump in with both feet? Make a commitment to yourself that you will make a series of beaded pieces that visually describe your experiences and feelings. Set your own "rules" using the following questions as guidelines.

What element (or elements) appeals to you enough so that you can keep it constant while working in series? Some possibilities are size, shape, theme, subject, technique, materials, color and design.

What specific number of pieces (or time period) will you make a commitment to do? What is realistic for you to accomplish?

Since this is a self-commitment, what will you do/feel if you fall behind? What are some ways to keep yourself motivated? Some possibilities are finding some bead buddies to do this with you, stating your commitment in writing, posting your process and progress on the web or rewarding yourself in a significant way for each piece you complete.

Tips

Be gentle with yourself.
Let go of trying to be perfect.
Try to forget about "figuring it out" and "getting it right."
Feel free to make mistakes.
Let your fingers, heart and inner child have a chance to express themselves.
Give yourself permission to tell your truth, even if it is difficult or unpleasant.
Let your inner critic take a vacation while you're working on your journal.
Think of your work as practice rather than a championship game.

You may find yourself rewarded with work that is unique and compelling, and with a greater understanding of yourself as an artist.

R. Atkins, 2007

Respect

6" x 4", Bead Journal Project, October, #5 in a series of 12 pieces

Telling Your Life Story

Notice and honor your everyday intelligence.
Feel the joy of being your own person.

I can't recall exactly what prompted me to tell my life story with beads, decade by decade. Yet I remember very clearly how compelling and exciting the process was, how I didn't want to do anything else during that time and how, as a result, I am a changed person.

Of course, you could attempt to tell your story in a single piece, perhaps a montage. But for me it seemed reasonable to take it a decade at a time, beading one piece for each 10-year period of my life.

I began by writing a timeline, a chronological outline of significant events and branching points in my life. After listing these, I identified some passions and issues that were important during certain periods. I color-coded my list, one color per decade.

At some point, while thus reviewing my life, I visualized a string of cut-out paper dolls and remembered making and playing with this form as a child. Thus I chose this doll form as the consistent shape for each piece.

Vowing to check my written timeline only once before starting to bead a given decade, I put the list in the back of my mind and began beading without further attention to it. I wanted to tell my life story improvisationally, without thinking about it very much, without planning or visualizing the outcome.

Now here is a confession. My third decade, ages 21 to 30, was a mess. My inner critic looked back at those aimless, irresponsible, drinking years with loathing and disgust. I could not bring myself (for a long time) to bead that decade. So I skipped it, beading from decade two to decades four and five.

Finally, a good friend said to me, "It's time to face the music. You just have to do it." And so, with great insecurity and fear, I began. You can see how it turned out on the next page.

R. Atkins, 2005

Decade Doll #3

4.5" x 4"
This doll represents my life story from ages 21 through 30.

Here's what I learned. My life those 10 years was a mess, yes. But it was also exciting, fun, adventurous, free, bold and educational in a nontraditional way. By the time my beading was complete, I didn't despise myself for that decade anymore. This blessing was completely unexpected, yet I know that working in series like this, and especially working improvisationally, can open our hearts and heal our wounds.

Looking at all six dolls on the cover, what do you see? Do they tell you anything about me? Can you guess at some of the events, passions, stories? Unlike a written autobiography, a beaded life story will always be a little ambiguous to the viewer. However, the important thing is in the telling of it, the process and feeling the joy of being your own person.

Try This

Bead your own life story.

Start by making a list or timeline of the following:
- significant events or turning points
- family
- births and deaths
- life's work
- your health history
- sexual identity
- your spiritual and philosophical life
- role of money
- passions, goals and aspirations

When you finish the list, give yourself time to think about how you might want to tell your story. Will it be as a whole, a montage of everything? Will you divide it into categories such as childhood, school years, marriage, children, working and retirement? Will you divide it into chronological time periods?

Give some thought to a shape for each piece (or the whole thing). What is a significant shape in your life? Some possibilities include house, heart, circle, spiral and triangle. If you can, find a shape that speaks in some way to all the chapters of your life.

Start anywhere, with any event or time period that feels right. You do not have to work chronologically unless that appeals to you.

Incorporate ephemera or mementos from your past. For example, you might use fabric from your old baby clothes or blanket as the background for beading about your childhood.

What about your school years? What have you kept that you could include in your piece? Do you have any memorbelia, ticket stubs, jewelry or buttons that remind you of a significant event? Use them in your work. You might also scan portions of important photographs, print them on fabric and incorporate them in your work.

Sometimes you may want to think about how to convey a certain event in a visually obvious way. Another method is to tuck that event in the back of your mind, sewing with beads and materials you love. Often, without benefit of your thinking mind, your heart and hands will reveal the important message from the event.

Be mindful, as you work on this project, that it is a huge and amazing experience to honor and record your life in this way. You may find yourself a little more emotional than usual during the process. Be gentle with yourself, take breaks when you need them, feel and be with the truths of your life, allow mistakes and imperfections. It's all good.

R. Atkins, 2005

Decade Doll #1

4.5" x 4"
This dolls tells the story of my life from birth through age 10. The dark vertical line represents the death of my biological father. My brother and I were sent to live with our grandparents while my mother returned to school. Two years with no Dad and an absent Mom were a little grim. But then Mom remarried and family love slowly grew and blossomed once again.

R. Atkins, 2008

Self-portrait

6" x 4", Bead Journal Project, January, #8 in a series of 12 pieces

Self-portrait

*In your search for self,
look beyond your image in the mirror
and touch your exquisitely innocent, inner being.*

For centuries, painters, sculptors and photographers have used self-portraits to explore a basic question: Who am I? They have gazed into a mirror and attempted to grasp a sense of their own identity and purpose in the world.

What do artists find when they search the mirror? For some the self-portrait is a cathartic experience, a letting-go of pent-up emotions. For others, the process reveals new insights about themselves and their work. For all artists, the self-portrait is a journey of self-exploration, an opportunity to see beyond the image in the mirror and begin a search into the inner soul.

I believe beading a self-portrait is a challenging, rewarding and self-actualizing experience. During the meditative process of sewing bead by bead, we may begin to acknowledge and accept ourselves as artists.

If you search "self-portrait" images on the internet, you will find many possibilities, ranging from the classic, posed torso of many early painters and photographers to entirely abstract representations (such as the one on the left) with no visual clues as to physical body parts. As beaders, we have this same range of expression.

Try This

To bead a classic self-portrait, begin with a photograph of your head and shoulders. Either transfer the photo to fabric or bead right over the photo itself. Select a spot on the photo that seems the most compelling. Matching the color and highlight/shadow, sew a single bead in this spot. Using back stitch or couching stitch, and matching the colors as you go, sew concentric circles of beads around this spot until the entire surface is beaded.[1]

---

[1] For more information about this method of beading, see *Beaded Embellishment* by Amy C. Clarke & Robin Atkins, ISBN #1-931499-12-8, pages 59-61 and 95-96.

To bead a more abstract self-portrait, begin with fabric and beads you love. Contemplate yourself, how you look, your passions, your personality, your hopes. Tuck these thoughts in the back of your mind, pick up a bead you love and sew it somewhere on your fabric. Without conscious attempts to represent yourself, continue to sew on beads you love until the portrait seems finished.[2]

Passions

Trust your dreams and your imagination.
There is always something available to you.

When we tap into our passions and use them in our art, we delight in every stitch we make. Our work has great credibility. We are compelled to finish. Our bead embroidery can be a way to celebrate, acknowledge and thank the universe for things we feel passionate about. Also, it can be a way to explore and understand our passions and our dreams.

Try This

Think about things, events, places, people and causes that have seemed extremely important at one time or another in your life. Try not to judge your thoughts. They may range from simple (like the color purple) to momentous (like the birth of your child). Let your thoughts percolate for a while, then write them all down.

Circle the one that seems the most compelling to you right now. With the circled passion in mind, select fabric and beads for your next project.

At this point, fear sometimes gets in our way. I've seen this in students and in myself. We begin to worry that we won't be able to do our passion justice, that our technical and artistic skills may not be good enough to be worthy of our great dream. We get stuck in this place of fear. We procrastinate, change our mind about the fabric a dozen times, take up knitting or go shopping for more beads.

---

[2] For more information about improvisational bead embroidery, see *One Bead at a Time* by Robin Atkins, ISBN #0-9705538-2-X.

Try to recognize fear behind procrastination, and don't let yourself give in to it. Take the pressure off; tell yourself it's OK to be average. Remind yourself you don't need to make anything perfect. Stay with your work, pick up a bead you love and sew it on your piece.

Another way that we get stuck is to hold our work up to our passion, finding fault with our work in comparison. Wanting our art to be as great as our passion is a natural tendency. However, it's easier to keep beading when we think of our art as being inspired by our passion rather than equaling it.

When you finish your piece, you will see that it is not the same as the dream or passion. It has its own value. The value may be in giving you a deeper appreciation and understanding of your dreams. Or, it may take you in a slightly new direction. Either way, because it began with something compelling to you, there will be a delightful sense of authenticity about it.

R. Atkins, 2005

Decade Doll #5

4.5" x 4"
This doll celebrates the passion I had during my 40's for folk dancing, folk music and folk art. For example, during that decade I attended folk art camps in Hungary, performed folk dance on many stages, studied native Siberian bead embroidery and learned several types of Transylvanian folk embroidery and beading. My whole life revolved around this abiding passion. Can you see it in this doll?

People You Love

*Creating a likeness of someone you love will give you
a precious sense of nearness and involvement with them.*

Beading portraits of people you love is fun and engaging. Whether the portrait is a realistic likeness or abstract, it is challenging to get under the skin of the person, to reveal something of the essence of their character.

To meet this challenge, I'm more successful when I work improvisationally, without a plan. I simply tuck all the feelings and knowledge I have of the person in the back of my mind, select some beads and a piece of fabric I love, and start beading. The less I think about it, the more my heart and hands are able to express about the person.

For example, to the right is a portrait of my mother, which I did improvisationally. What can you see about her character? Notice how rooted she is, how love flows into her big heart, expanding as she gives it back to her family and the world, and how she has a strong inner flame of strength. If I had beaded her face, perhaps using a photograph as a guide, could I have shown these things? Certainly it would have been more difficult.

Try This

Once I had the opportunity to participate in a group therapy session where we drew other-handed portraits of people we love. This might be a good starting point for a beaded piece about someone you love.

Get out some crayons or colored markers and a sheet of paper. Think for a moment about a person you love. In the next three to five minutes, use your non-dominant hand to draw a portrait of this person. That is, if you're right-handed, draw with your left hand and vice versa. Do not draw eyes, nose, ears, hair, etc. Use color, lines and shapes to convey your feelings and knowledge about this person. If you have one, set a timer for three minutes. Re-set the timer for two more minutes if you need more time to complete your drawing.

Use the drawing as a guide to bead your portrait. This may require a certain amount of trust. As you bead, feel free to add other elements or colors as needed to further illuminate this person's character and your unique relationship with them.

R. Atkins, 1994

Mom's Pouch

5.5" x 5.75"
The bead embroidery on this pouch
is an abstract "picture" of my mother.

Places You Love

*Reveal your deep inner yearnings
for your most cherished place in this world,
and I will give you my rapt attention.*

For always and always, painters and photographers have given us glimpses of their favorite places on earth—fields of sunflowers, mountains and villages, rivers and oceans, the streets of Paris. It only makes sense that we beaders can portray our most adored places as well.

My first piece celebrating a special place didn't start out with any subject at all. It began with beads and fabric I love, but no pre-conceived plan or concept. As I sewed beads on the fabric, it started to remind me of our five-acre property in the spring when all the little wildflowers bloom and abundant mosses in every possible shade of green carpet the rocks. Once that thought occurred to me, I allowed the piece to take shape and further cultivated the likeness to our property. I even included my studio, which is about 50 yards up a trail from our house. I call the finished, framed piece *Moss & Wildflowers* (see right).

My next piece of this type was a commission for a woman who said she wanted a landscape, but other than that I could have complete freedom to bead as I wished. "Freedom" being music to my ears, I selected fabric and beads I loved and started to work, again without a clue as to the outcome. The only thing I did was tuck the word "landscape" in the back of my mind. Soon, the jagged, snow-covered peaks, river valleys and rolling lowland hills of the Cascade Mountains began to emerge. Add a waterfall, blue skies, wind—and you have one of my favorite places in the world!

Here (page 30) you can see this piece when it was about one third complete. By that time, I knew where it was going. Next to it (page 31) is the finished piece, which I framed and sent to my customer.

Both of these pieces were extremely pleasing to make. Although both of them are large and solidly beaded, I was never bored or restless while working on them. I believe that's partly because they weren't pre-designed, and even more importantly because they represent places I love passionately.

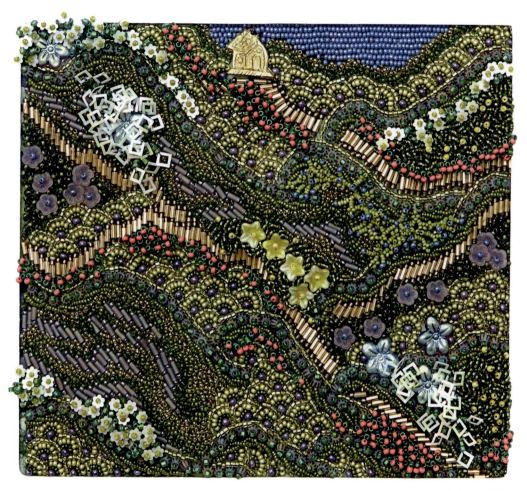

R. Atkins, 2000

Moss & Wildflowers

6" x 6.5"

This piece represents springtime on our five-acre, ridgetop property,
when wildflowers bloom abundantly and mosses in every hue of green carpet the rocks.

Try This

Make a small piece suggesting a detail of a place that's very special to you. Try to capture the essence of this place in a piece about three by four inches, or smaller. For this one piece, try the improvisational approach. Select a piece of fabric and beads that remind you in some way of your chosen place. Begin sewing beads without a clue about how it will look when it is complete. Finish the piece no matter what and mount it in a shadow box or small frame. Hang it where you will see it often and note how much it pleases you day after day.

R. Atkins, 2005

Mountains & Streams

6.5" x 6", about one third completed

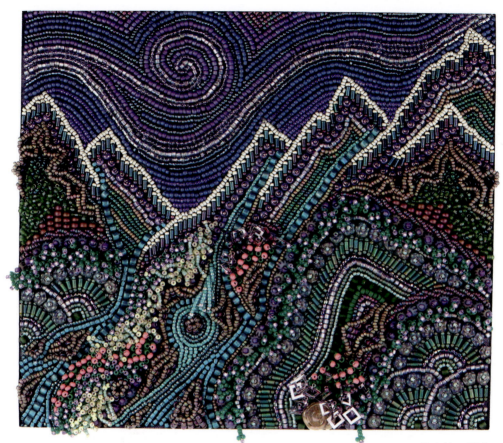

R. Atkins, 2005

Mountains & Streams

6" x 6.5"

The person who commissioned me to do this piece requested that I bead a landscape of my choice. Having spent countless, glorious, summer days hiking in the nearby Cascade and Olympic Mountains, it's not surprising that these giant, craggy, glacier-covered peaks and verdant, lowland hills emerged as the subject of my beading.

Things You Love

Show me your love for a dark and thorny thing,
and through your eyes, I will see its beauty and purpose.

One day while waiting for an appointment, I started writing a list of everything I love. At the top of the list were obvious things such as kittens, winter wrens, rainbows, bunny rabbits, Madrona trees, red shoes, glass beads, the Aurora Borealis, chocolate, etc. Then I found myself adding somewhat unexpected things, such as bridges, pebbles, tiny containers, coffee, silk scarves and the Blues. This list is a blessing, because it opens many inspirational doors for my bead embroidery.

Try This

Give yourself half an hour of peace and quiet to write a list of things you love. Get wild and crazy with this list! Write as quickly as you can, without any judgments about any of the items on the list. You can always cross them out or burn the whole list later.

Circle the one thing on the list that seems the most compelling at this moment. That is the subject for your next bead embroidery. Look at it as an experiment, challenging yourself to show your passion as deeply as possible.

Causes & Concerns

When you believe in a thing with all your heart,
leap into the experience of it every way you can.

In recent years, bead quilts have become popular auction items to raise funds for breast cancer research and other causes. Artists donate beaded squares, which volunteers then assemble. I believe participating in group fundraisers like this and donating finished work to worthy causes are good things to do. I also know that creating art inspired by our belief in a cause helps us to understand it and to feel more empowered.

Whether we are concerned about far-reaching, global issues or local problems, I believe we can use our bead embroidery to put a positive force toward solution into the universe. As we stitch in a mindful, perhaps prayerful way, we imbue our art with our caring energy. This, in turn, is felt by those who see our work and, through the ripple effect, by the whole world.

For example, the Madrona trees of the Pacific Northwest have been increasingly stressed by higher temperatures and less rain in the past decade. Since we have many of these lovely trees on our property, their cause is close to my heart. I've made two spirit dolls[3], each filled with respectful prayers. The energy of one is directed toward the trees themselves, the other toward increased rainfall in the shoulder seasons (see pages 34 and 35).

Without quite understanding how or why it works, I believe my steady trickle of positive energy about this concern joins an affirmative flow from countless other hearts toward change for the better.

Try This

Identify a concern you may have for the well-being of the world, mankind, the universe. Select fabric and beads you love. Plan your piece or work improvisationally (or some combination). With every stitch and every bead, give of your heart. Write your prayers on the back (or the front) of your piece. Imagine your voice joining the voices of others.

Take a chance. Find an organization that recognizes and is trying to do something about your concern. Contact them about your piece. Maybe they hold fund-raising auctions. Maybe they will photograph it for their newsletter or website. Your voice, speaking through your bead embroidery, can make a difference.

---

[3] For more information about making bead-embellished dolls for healing, guidance, protection, friendship, remembering and celebration, see *Spirit Dolls* by Robin Atkins, ISBN #0-9705538-4-6.

Madrona

9" x 4.25"
It is my prayer that the energy
in this spirit doll will protect and
nourish the Madrona trees,
which are found only in the Pacific
Northwest. They are suffering
from the effects of decreasing
shoulder-season rainfall.

R. Atkins, 2005

Aqua

9" x 4.25"
A companion piece to *Madrona* (opposite page), the energy in this spirit doll is directed toward plentiful rain and water conservation efforts.

R. Atkins, 2007

Personal Issues

*Through creative work with our hands,
we are allowed a visit to the inner world of our soul,
the home of understanding and healing.*

For the past 20 years, I've intentionally used improvisational bead embroidery to find resolution, forgiveness, healing and understanding about my own personal issues. If you have no unresolved matters in your life, feel free to skip this chapter. If you can identify a question to be answered, a problem to be solved, a hurt to be soothed, a behavior to be changed, a relationship to be improved, or any such issue affecting your enjoyment of life, sewing beads on fabric can be a huge help. Often, the resulting work is both compelling and healing to others as well.

The act of stitching itself, the meditative process of beading, provides therapeutic benefits to many who do it. And when we deliberately begin a piece with a specific issue in mind, these benefits are even greater. It doesn't matter whether we work improvisationally, without any pre-conceived plan, or by following a carefully designed idea. Either way, as our hands stitch beads, our hearts begin to open and speak to us with gentle compassion.

To illustrate two ways of approaching personal issues with bead embroidery, I will share with you the process of making two of my Bead Journal Project (see page 15) pieces.

Four months before my 65th birthday, I became somewhat anxious and depressed at the prospect of starting Medicare and facing life as a senior citizen. This became the focus of my bead embroidery for June. I decided to work improvisationally without a clue as to how or what I would bead, an approach that always works well for me.

Tucking my issue about age in the back of my mind, I sorted through my fabric stash until scraps from two previous projects attracted my attention. I placed one scrap (the waste fabric from cutting out a doll) on top of the other and then machine stitched them both to a piece of paper (stabilizer), sewing along the lines of the doll shape and around the outside stitch guide marked on the paper.

R. Atkins, 2007

Facing a Wall of Denial

6" x 4", Bead Journal Project, June, #1 in a series of 12 pieces

Picking up a permanent ink pen, I wrote a brief journal entry right there on my piece. Here's what it says:

> *I am facing a wall of denial. I don't want to accept my age. I don't want to be a senior citizen. Youth and youthfulness. I can't go back. The clock keeps ticking. It's a wall.*

Since, at the time, I thought I might cover my words with beads, it didn't concern me that the ink bled into the fabric or that my writing was so candid. Now, in retrospect, I'm happy that I didn't bead over these words (see page 37).

Next, I filled a small box with beads that appealed to me at that moment, and started to stitch the number 65 with yellow beads. The face-bead for an eye (looking at 65) and the clock bead followed.

Now what? "Pick up a bead you love and sew it on somewhere." That's what I always say to my students, so that is what I did. Blue, green, pink, purple, red and orange beads formed a patchwork square. Where there's a square, there must be a triangle, a circle, a cross and a spiral. Right? I guess so, because that's what happened next, followed by a winding orange line connecting everything. What does it mean? While I'm beading, I try not to ask.

Today when I look at the piece, I think the red fabric represents the wall of denial, right there in front of my face. Look what's beyond it. Flowers! When I see my big, warm heart, all those pretty flowers beyond the wall and the pathway through the wall that is my life, how can I not feel better about turning 65? Working on this piece helped me to switch from an attitude of denial to one of integrating the past with the future, of accepting who I am.

A few months later, another personal issue surfaced. This time it was worry about finances, the economy and having enough money in the future. My husband frequently tells me, "It's only money." So I decided to see if beading a piece about money might help. What better way, I thought, than to use a $100 bill in my piece! Wouldn't that be a great way to let it go?

This piece was planned to a certain extent before I began working on it. I envisioned torn money with the mighty power of the tiger holding the "door" through the money open for me and the gentle spirit of the rabbit to ease the journey. With this idea in mind, I began to bead the tiger first (see page 39).

It's Only Money

6" x 4", Bead Journal Project, August, #3 in a series of 12 pieces

Trying to tell myself, "It's only money" had never worked for me. Beading the message on a hundred dollar bill and including the power of tiger and nurturing of rabbit has significantly modified my thinking and my behavior around financial worrying.

Without going into details about why, Christmas has always been a tough (dark and upside down) time for me. This too became the subject of an "attitude changing" piece (page 41).

Try This

Identify something that is troubling to you, such as a decision you've been trying to make or a behavior you'd like to change. State the issue in simple terms. In the examples here, I used the words *age*, *money* and *Christmas*, respectively, to sum up all aspects of my problem attitudes. Commit to making a piece of bead embroidery around that issue.

Whether to plan or to work improvisationally is up to you. Gather some beads and fabric. If possible, choose fabric that is somehow related to the issue. For example, if your relationship with your mother is troubling you, consider beading on fabric that was once a garment she wore, or one she made for you or gave to you.

With a permanent ink pen, scribble a few words and phrases about your issue on the paper stabilizer or directly on the fabric. Do this quickly and try to state only true facts without including judgments or condemnations.

As you begin beading, let yourself experiment and play. Giver yourself permission to be just average. Decide that it's OK if you don't know how it will all turn out. Sew beads on your fabric with great abandon. Allow yourself time and privacy to work as much as you want on this piece. Resolve that this piece will not be for sale or exhibition, that it will not be a gift and that it doesn't have to please anybody. Lift the pressure off yourself to be creative or perfect. This is your time to find yourself and resolve what has been troubling you through the work of your hands. So give them freedom and permission to work.

During the process, resist the temptation to analyze your work and your choices. There will be time enough for that when you finish. And you will know when you are finished. Sometimes you feel the sense of completion and resolution even before the fabric is covered with beads. Sometimes it takes more than one piece.

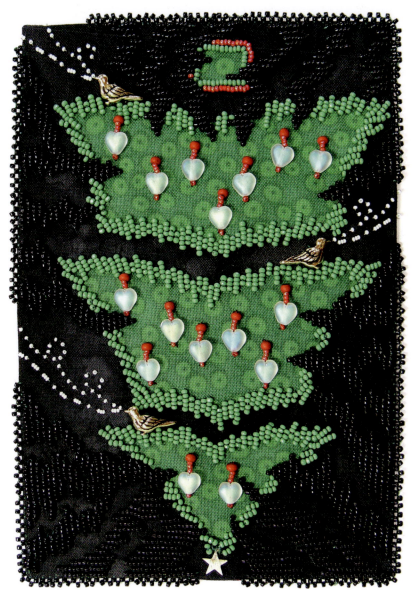

R. Atkins, 2007

Dark Thoughts Pointing at Christmas

6" x 4", Bead Journal Project, December, #7 in a series of 12 pieces

Tributes and Memorials

When you grieve with colors and shapes, beads and fibers, you can say things that can't be said with words.

When we are suffering the loss of a family member, friend, pet or even an important life goal, we understand that memory—remembering the good times and the past events of our shared lives—is important. One way to focus on positive memories is to create a visual tribute and record of our relationship to the one who has perished. Such a tribute can be an effective tool to help us understand our emotional path and also to provide a meaningful reminder for years to come.

I have beaded the loss of my Daddy[4], who died when I was five years old, my dear stepfather, who died in 2006, the destruction of the twin towers in New York City, women who have died from breast cancer and my beautiful cat, Mia. Each time, my grief, despair, love, anger and lost feelings pour out of me. With every bead and every stitch, I am surrounded by a deeper sense of the lost one. A seed of connection grows and begins to flourish. Grief and sorrow are joined by delight and truth.

My tribute to Mia (fondly known as *Miss Mia Maria Rotundus Abundus*) began during her extended illness. Aware that her remaining life would be measured in months, I began a piece of bead embroidery (page 43, lower left) as a tribute to her. Although I tried to imbue it with healing thoughts, part of me understood that soon she would be gone. I stitched with love and with sadness.

After she died, I finished beading, gathered poems I had written about her, pictures, a card with a kitty-angel drawn by a neighbor who also loved her, a beaded kitty button made by a friend who understands how much we love our pets and a sterling kitty, made by a jeweler friend with the same understanding. I collaged these loving reminders of Mia in a shadow box (page 43), which stands on a window sill in my studio. Every time I'm there, I see the tribute, remember her and feel a connection with her.

---

[4] See *One Bead at a Time, Exploring Creativity with Bead Embroidery* by Robin Atkins, ISBN #0-9705538-2-X, pages 31-35.

R. Atkins, 2000

Miss Mia Maria

10" x 8"

Grieving the tragedy of 9-11[5], Andrea Adams needed to express her feelings with her beads. Reading various bead lists and forums, she noticed others with the same need and posted her budding idea as follows: "I would like to do something with my beadwork, as that's how I process my emotions. Maybe a large beaded quilt, with 'squares' from many different beadworkers? I don't know, I haven't really thought it through... but the idea came to me, and I'm wondering if anyone else would have interest in some sort of project like this...? As I said before, I believe that creating beadwork can be a healing process, and I like to think that the results of that creative energy can have some healing effects as well."

Quickly beaders around the country (and in several foreign countries) took up their needles and beads to create three-inch squares. As the squares started pouring in, so did the volunteer offers of help. A team of 27 women formed to coordinate this project, the first and largest of its kind, before or since. There are 573 squares pictured on the official Bead Quilt website. Some are bead embroidery, some are woven and all of them are powerful and amazing. Who can say what the collective, long-term effects of creating this quilt might be?

While my emotions were still very raw, I beaded a square for the quilt (page 45), honoring the missing twin towers and those who were lost within them. Without a doubt, the meditative process of stitching beads on my square helped to take my thoughts away from death, destruction and rubble and guide them toward light, caring and peace.

Beading memorials and tributes is a way of embracing our pain, preserving our memories and staying connected. In my experience, it is also a way of expressing what I feel in a way that I could never manage with words. If you are experiencing grief over an old or new loss, I encourage you to pick up your needle and get to work.

Try This

Gather mementos and pictures, anything you have that triggers your memories. Find a fabric that reminds you of (or once belonged to) the subject of your tribute. You do not have to plan your work, know how it will be used or how you'll display it when it's finished. With your subject in mind, your beading will begin to take shape.

---

[5] Terrorist attacks of September 11, 2001.

Empty Spaces

3" x 3"
I made this square for the 9-11 Bead Quilt Project. It depicts the fallen twin towers and honors those who were lost within them.

R. Atkins, 2001

As you stitch beads, memories will surface and flow through your mind. You may experience doubt that your work will be worthy of your subject. Try not to let your fears of inadequacy stop you. Perfection is not necessary to memory. If it helps, decide that you will not show your work to anybody. You may also experience uncomfortable emotions, such as anger. As part of your truth regarding your loss, it's OK to let your feelings show in your work.

As with other beadwork based on life experiences, the process (the wisdom, understanding and acceptance that develop while stitching bead by bead) is the most important outcome of your work. I'm guessing that, on the average, at least 80 percent of the benefit is from creating the piece. Beyond that, what you do with it (embellish a photo album cover or urn, frame it or just keep it in a special place) doesn't matter as much as you might think.

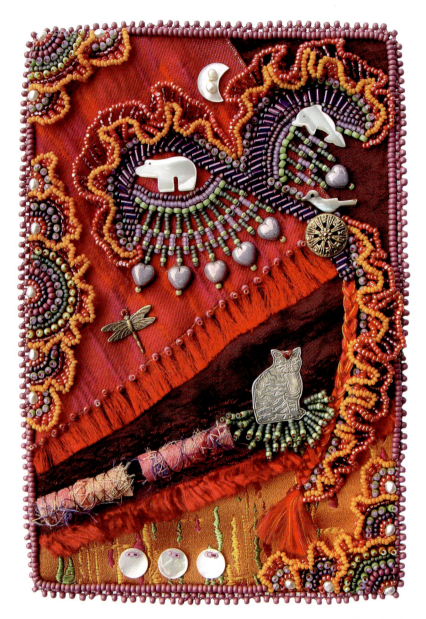

R. Atkins, 2007

Gifts

6" x 4", Bead Journal Project, September, #4 in a series of 12 pieces

Techniques

We began this book with ideas and suggestions for creating unique, personal and engaging beadwork. The pages which follow will introduce you to 20 bead embroidery techniques that I particularly enjoy using in my work. Have fun playing with them! Each technique is illustrated with a sample and, whenever possible, with a detail picture from finished bead embroidery pieces. By experimenting with these techniques—altering the size, spacing and color of beads—you can develop your own variations to suit your specific needs.

Decade Doll #2

4.5" x 4"
This doll represents my life story from ages 11 through 20. Techniques used here include short stacks, twisted fringe, barnacles and wildflowers, all of which are shown in the following pages.

R. Atkins, 2005

Tall & Short Stacks

Stacks add raised texture and definition to bead embroidery. There are many variations of stacks, including lines of short stacks and clusters of tall stacks such as those shown in the sample piece for this technique. Stacks form the basis of several fancy techniques that follow.

Short stacks are made with two beads. I like to use a larger bead (size 5 or 8) for the bottom bead of the stack, and a smaller bead (size 11 or 15) for the top bead of the stack.

To make a short stack, sew to the beading side of your fabric. Pick up a larger bead followed by a smaller bead. Slide both beads along the thread to the surface of the fabric. Sew back through the hole of the larger bead and through the fabric to the wrong side. When you snug the thread tension, you will notice that the smaller bead sits on top of the larger bead.

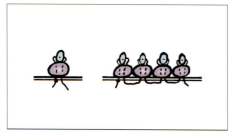

fig. 1
Make lines of short stacks, each two beads high.

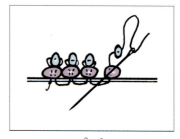

fig. 2
Alter stack placement.

To make a line of short stacks, bring the needle to the surface near the first stack and repeat the steps above for making a short stack (fig 1). You can adjust the placement of any stack on the return trip through the bottom bead of the stack. Use the needle to move the stack into the desired position as you sew into the fabric (fig. 2). Repeat these steps to make curved or straight lines of any length.

On the sample (page 48), notice lines of short stacks making a Y-shape in the center, a curve in the lower right corner and the curve at the center top. These were made with size 8 for the bottom bead and size 15 for the top bead in each stack. Lines like this, formed with short stacks, tend to be a prominent design element.

Tall stacks are made with three or more beads. I generally use relatively small beads (size 8, 11 or 15) for the bottom beads of the stack and either the same size or smaller for the top bead of the stack.

To make a tall stack, sew to the beading side of your fabric. Pick up two or more beads on your needle followed by whatever bead you want to use for the top bead of the stack. Slide all of the beads to the surface of your fabric. Skipping the top bead, sew back through the remainder of the beads in the stack and then through the fabric to the wrong side (fig. 3, left).

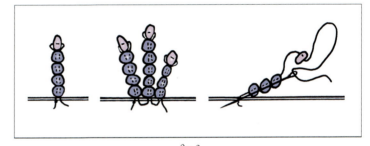

fig. 3
Tall stacks (three or more beads high) may be single or clustered. Sew at an angle to make stacks lay close to surface of the fabric.

To make a cluster of tall stacks, bring the needle to the surface near the first stack and repeat the steps above for making a tall stack. Repeat these steps several more times (fig. 3, center). Like short stacks, the placement of a tall stack can be adjusted slightly as you sew through the bottom bead of the stack and into the fabric.

The relative stiffness of taller stacks (six or more beads high) can be controlled with thread tension. To make stiff, spiky stacks, pull the thread snug on the back side and knot after each stack. The direction that the top of the stack points can be controlled slightly with the direction of the needle's path through the fabric. To make a stack that "sprays" to the right of its starting point (fig. 3. right), bring the needle to the surface at an angle pointing right. Make the stack and return the needle to the fabric at an angle pointing left. On the sample, notice there are two clusters of tall stacks, one in the center of the top curve and one on the far left. Also along the left side, there is a line of tall stacks next to the line of short stacks.

Barnacles

This raised form suggests different things depending on the size, colors and spacing of the beads used to construct it. One might see a sea creature, as the name implies, a flower center, a breast, a volcano or even a towering structure in a city. Of course, it's also a lovely textural element in a more abstract piece such as the sample to the left.

To make a barnacle, you'll need a small circle of identical stacks, five or six beads tall. It works nicely to use three sizes of beads. Use size 8 for the bottom bead, size 11 for the middle beads and size 15 for the top bead of each stack. Although you will achieve a slightly different look, you can also make barnacles using only one or two different sizes of beads.

Visualize (or mark) a circle slightly smaller than a dime on your fabric. Beginning anywhere on the circumference of the circle, make a tall stack five or six beads high (page 49). Make another, identical stack right next to the first one. Continue making identical stacks all the way around the circle.

After completing the last stack in the circle, you'll be on the wrong side. From here, sew through the fabric and up through the beads in stack number one including its top bead. Your thread now exits the top bead of stack number one (fig. 4). From this position, sew through the top bead of stack number two. Continue sewing through just the top bead of

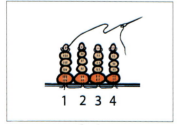

fig. 4
Thread at top bead of first stack.

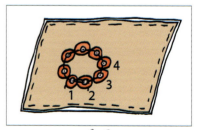

fig. 5
Join the top beads of all stacks.

each stack until you've gone all the way around the circle. Sew through the top bead of stack number one a second time. Sew down through all the beads in stack number two and through the fabric to the wrong side (fig. 5). Pull the thread snug and make a knot to secure the tension.

The circle may be larger or smaller and the number of beads in each stack more or less than suggested above. You may need to experiment a bit to get the look you wish to achieve.

R. Atkins, 2005

Mountains & Streams

6" x 6.5", detail (See entire piece on page 31.)
There are four barnacles used to represent land forms in this piece.
Notice that one large, irregularly-shaped barnacle has a smaller one inside of it.

Bezels

A bezel is a raised edge or rim that circles a cabochon and holds it in place on the surface of your bead embroidery. A cabochon is an element that is domed on the top and flat on the bottom. We can make a beaded bezel using tall stacks joined together at the top. Although there are other ways to make beaded bezels, this way is both easy to learn and flexible for use with irregularly shaped cabochons.

The first step to making a beaded bezel is to secure the cabochon on the beading surface. Although some artists use glue or double-stick tape for this purpose, I prefer to hold it in place with removable stitches that pass over the top of the cabochon in a web.

Using the same thread as for beading, sew to the surface of the fabric next to the cabochon (temporarily held in place with your thumb). Sew down into the fabric on the other side of the cabochon, come to the surface and sew across again forming an X with the two stitches. Come to the surface again in a different place around the edge of the cabochon and cross to the other side. On the fourth stitch over the top of the cabochon, take an extra little stitch around the threads at the point where the previous stitches cross each other (fig. 6). Continue in this manner until the cabochon is firmly secured in place.

Once it is secured, follow the steps for making a barnacle (pages 50-51) to circle the cabochon with tall stacks. The height of the stacks depends on the height and size of the required bezel. The stacks must be tall enough to draw inward onto the dome of the cabochon when the tops are joined. If the dome is uneven, vary the height of the stacks as needed (fig. 7). Generally I use only one size of beads to make the stacks for a bezel. Unless it's a very large cabochon, I tend to use size 15 beads.

When the cabochon is circled, sew up through the beads in the first stack, and from there join the top beads of all the stacks, the same as for a barnacle (fig. 5, page 50). Sew through the top bead of the first stack a second time and then down through the beads of the second stack. Pull the thread snug on the back side. Check the bezel to be sure that it's tight and that no thread is showing between the top beads. If it looks good, knot on the back side.

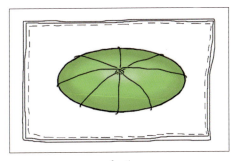 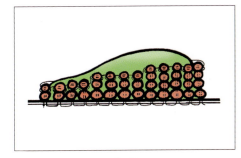

fig. 6
Temporary stitches hold cabochon in place.

fig. 7
Stack height depends on crest of cabochon.

If there is thread showing, observe carefully and estimate how many extra top beads it will take to fill the gaps. Remove your needle and pull out the thread that joins all the top beads. Re-sew through the top beads, only this time add the estimated number of extra beads, spacing them evenly around the circumference. Check again to make sure the bezel is tight and that there is no thread showing. Repeat adjustment if necessary. Knot on the back side when it looks good. To complete the bezel, clip the temporary stitches where they cross (on top of the cabochon) and remove them.

As an extra precaution, especially for larger or heavier cabochons, double secure the bezel. After adjusting and knotting off the bezel, sew up through the beads of any stack to the top, sew through the top beads of all the stacks a second (sometimes even a third) time, then sew down through the beads of a stack to the back side, and knot again.

R. Atkins, 2007

Respect

6" x 4", Bead Journal Project, October, detail (See entire piece on page 17.)

Half Shells

I call this raised form a half shell, but it can also look like the moon, a land form or a basket depending on the size, color and spacing of the beads used. Imagine fancy fringe pouring out of this form, or using it to partly hide a bead or button sewn in the center of it!

Envision or mark (page 10) a half circle on your fabric. Make a line of tall stacks (page 49) along the half circle. For each stack, use graduated sizes of beads, starting with the largest (size 6 or 8) on the bottom and topping each stack with the smallest (size 15). The stacks are also graduated in height. Make the stacks toward the middle of the half circle about double the height of the stacks on both ends (fig. 8).

After completing a half circle of stacks, knot on the back side. Then sew up through the beads of the last stack you made and join the top bead of each stack (fig. 9). Sew down through the beads of the stack at the other end of the half circle and into the fabric. Snug the thread and knot on the back side.

A little experimenting with the spacing and height of the stacks, the size of the beads in each stack and the colors of the beads will yield many variations in the look of this form.

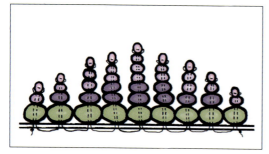

fig. 8
Graduate the stack heights.

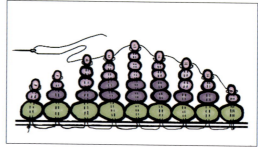

fig. 9
Join the top beads of all the stacks.

Spiral Shells

This raised, spiral form can look organic, like a real shell, or it can be more of an abstract design element. In one of my pieces, I used it to set and showcase a small cabochon face. The spiral is an archetypal symbol suggesting both an inward and outward mystical journey. By beading a three-dimensional spiral, the symbolic aspect of the form may be emphasized in your design.

Envision or mark (page 10) a spiral shape on your fabric. Make a curving line of short and tall stacks (pages 48-49) along the entire length of the spiral. For each stack, start with one or two larger beads on the bottom (size 11) and top each stack with smaller beads (size 15). The stacks must be graduated in height. Make the stacks toward the middle of the spiral at least triple the height of the stacks on both ends. For example, follow the chart below, adjusting the number of stacks as needed for the size of your spiral.

Step	Description of stacks in this step	Number of stacks
1	one size 11 bead + one size 15 bead (shortest stacks)	2
2	one size 11 bead + two size 15 beads	3
3	one size 11 bead + three size 15 beads	4
4	two size 11 beads + three size 15 beads	5
5	two size 11 beads + four size 15 beads	5
6	two size 11 beads + five size 15 beads	5
7	three size 11 beads + five size 15 beads (tallest stacks)	5
8	two size 11 beads + five size 15 beads	5
9	two size 11 beads + four size 15 beads	5
10	two size 11 beads + three size 15 beads	5
11	one size 11 bead + three size 15 beads	4
12	one size 11 bead + two size 15 beads	3
13	one size 11 bead + one size 15 bead (shortest stacks)	2

After completing the spiral of stacks, knot on the back side. Then sew up through the beads of the ending stack (closest to where you made the knot). From there, join the top bead of each stack until you reach the other end of the spiral. Sew down through the beads of the last stack and into the fabric. Snug the thread and knot on the back side.

A little experimenting with the spacing and height of the stacks, the size of the beads in each stack and the colors of the beads will yield many variations in the look of this form. As shown below, I sometimes use the spiral as a bezel to encase a carved face cabochon.

Detail showing face cabochon circled by a spiral shell.

R. Atkins, 2005

Decade Doll #6

4.5" x 4"

Ruffles

Ruffles are so much fun! They can add both texture and a sense of movement to your work. In one of my pieces, I used ruffles to suggest a party or celebration. In another, I used them to suggest land forms like cliffs or canyons. The sample to the right shows three side-by-side ruffles.

Envision or mark (page 10) a straight or curved line for one ruffle. Make a line of short and tall stacks (pages 48-49) along the entire length of the line. I tend to use one size of beads for these stacks. The stacks must be graduated in height. Make the stack at the start of the line two beads high. Increase the height of the stacks gradually to five (or more) beads high in the center of the line. Reverse this order for the other half of the line (fig. 10). After completing the line of stacks, knot on the back side.

To complete the ruffle, I generally use the same size and color of beads as the top beads on the stacks. This makes the wavy line of the ruffle appear continuous. Sew up through the fabric close to the last stack you made. Thread two beads on your needle and sew through the top bead of the last stack in the line. Then thread two beads on your needle and sew through the top bead of the next stack in the line (fig. 11). Continue in this way, adding one to three beads between the top beads of all the stacks. The more beads you add, the more ruffled it

fig. 10
Stacks are shorter at both ends of the line.

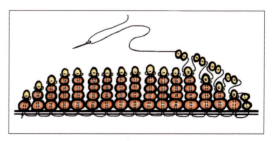

fig. 11
Add extra beads at both ends of the line and when joining the top beads.

will become. After passing through the top bead of the last stack, add two beads and sew into the fabric just beyond the last stack. Snug the thread and knot on the back side.

As shown in the sample (page 57) and the picture below, you can create an interesting effect by placing two or more ruffled lines side by side.

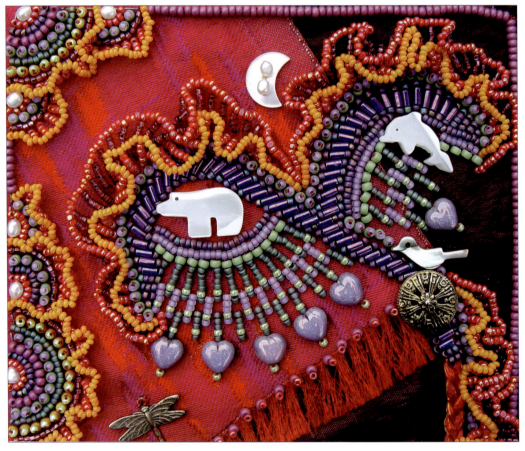

R. Atkins, 2007

Gifts

6" x 4", Bead Journal Project, September, detail (See entire piece on page 46.)

Flat Flowers

This flat, circular form can look like a flower (for example, a daisy), the sun, a wheel, a spider web, a sea urchin, or a nebula. Circles are archetypal symbols, representing wholeness and eternity. Beading flat circular forms may suggest meaning beyond the obvious representation.

As a first step, you may want to review the directions for making a barnacle (pages 50-51), because flat flowers are made the same way except for the spacing of the stacks.

Visualize or mark (page 10) a circle about three-quarters of an inch in diameter on your fabric. Make identical stacks, five or six beads tall, around the circle. It works nicely to use three sizes of beads, such as size 8 for the bottom bead, size 11 for the middle beads and size 15 for the top bead of each stack. The stacks should not touch one another. Space them evenly arund the circle, about one bead's width apart.

When the circle is complete, sew up through the beads in the first stack you made to the top. Sew from the top bead of stack number one through the top bead of stack number two. Continue sewing through just the top bead of each stack until you've gone all the way around the circle. Sew through the top bead of stack number one a second time. Sew down through all the beads in stack number two and through the fabric to the wrong side.

If the spacing is correct, all of the stacks will pull toward the center (like spokes of a wheel) and lay flat. Pull the thread snug and make a knot to secure the tension.

In the sample above, I added a bead in the center of each flower and short lines of small beads between each of the stacks after completing the form. Although you will achieve a slightly different look, you can use two or even just one size of beads to make the stacks. If the stacks are taller than the radius of the circle, the form will not lay flat. But that's OK. It will look more like a dome. By eliminating one or two stacks across the circle from each other, you can create a form that looks like a spider or other insect.

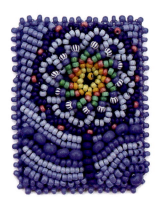

Pinwheel Flowers

This form is especially fun because it combines both the wholeness of a circle and the flowing movement of the spiral. It can be used to suggest a whirlpool, a child's toy and organic forms, such as the flower shown in the sample to the left.

As a first step, you may want to review the directions for making a barnacle (pages 50-51) and a flat flower (page 59), because pinwheels are made the same way except for a twist at the end of the process.

Visualize or mark (page 10) a circle about three-quarters of an inch in diameter on your fabric. Make identical stacks, eight beads tall, around the circle. It works nicely to use three sizes of beads, such as size 8 for the bottom bead, size 11 for the middle beads and size 15 for the top three beads of each stack. The stacks should not touch one another. Space them about one bead's width apart.

When the circle is complete, sew up through the beads in the first stack you made to the top. Sew from the top bead of stack number one through the top bead of stack number two. Continue sewing through just the top bead of each stack until you've gone all the way around the circle. Sew through the top bead of all the stacks a second time.

Do not sew through all the beads in the last stack and through the fabric to the wrong side as you would for a flat flower. Instead, make the pinwheel shape by pulling on the thread and using your fingers to twist the top of the stacks either clockwise or counter-clockwise. Sew into the fabric near the hub of the pinwheel to secure the twist. Bring your needle to the surface on the other side of the hub, and sew over the thread between two beads to couch it in place (see couching instructions on page 61). Repeat this process as necessary to secure the center of the pinwheel to the fabric.

In the sample (page 60), I added a bead in the center of the pinwheel and two rows of beads around the ends of the spokes, making it look more like a flower than a toy pinwheel.

Couching

Several of the techniques in this book require an understanding of couching. This over-hand type of stitch may be used to secure beading, fringe, fibers or cording to the beading surface. Another frequent use for couching is for adjusting the placement of a line of beads. For example, perhaps you've used backstitch to make the stem of a flower and the curve of it isn't smooth. You can use couching to move the section of the line that you don't like over a bit, adjusting it into a more pleasing curve.

Couching originated with thread embroidery and is used to fasten decorative cords to a fabric surface. First position the cord on the fabric as desired. Using a fine thread, sew from the back side to the surface next to one end of the cord. Sew over the top of the cord and back into the fabric just on the other side of the cord to form a single couching stitch. Repeat this process about every quarter of an inch or as needed to secure the cord in place.

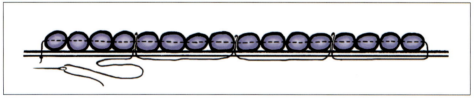

fig. 12
String beads and lay them in place on the fabric surface. Then, working back toward the start of the line, stitch over the top of the line, between two beads. Couch after every third to fifth bead.

Couching a curved or straight line of beads is the same, except that the thread that passes over the top of the line will not show. Sew from the back side to the surface next to a line of beads at a place where two beads touch. Sew over the top of the line of beads, passing the thread between the two beads, and back into the fabric just on the other side of the line. Repeat this process about every quarter of an inch or as needed to secure the line (fig. 12).

Raised Flowers

Use this method to create somewhat realistic flowers with three-dimensional petals. Although the sample to the left shows small flowers, each with only three or four petals, you can make more complex flowers using the same technique. By varying the colors of beads, you can add realistic shading detail to your beaded flowers.

Start with the flower center. This can be a short stack (page 48), a crystal, a pearl, a small, flower-shaped bead, etc. Sew the flower center on your fabric.

Basically, each petal is a short ruffle (pages 57-58). Use small seed beads, all the same size. For the first petal, make a short, curved line of stacks, which begins next to the flower center and gradually moves away from the center by about one bead's width. Like the ruffle, graduate the height of the stacks from two beads high to four or five beads high, and back down to two beads high.

After completing the line of stacks, knot on the back side. Then sew up through the fabric close to the last stack you made. Thread two beads on your needle and sew through the top bead of the last stack in the line. Then thread one bead on your needle and sew through the top bead of the next stack in the line. Continue in this way, adding one or two beads between each of the top beads (page 57, fig. 11). After passing through the top bead of the last stack, add two beads and sew into the fabric just beyond the last stack and next to the flower center. Snug the thread and knot on the back side.

In the same way, continue making petals around the flower center. Each petal starts just inside the previous petal (fig. 13). You can add another ring of petals outside the first, and as many more as you like. The petals can all be about the same size, as in a mum. Or, the petals can get larger on the outer rings, as in a rose.

fig. 13
Make curved lines of stacks around flower center.

Wildflowers

Small, raised dots of color provide a rich texture and depth to a beaded surface. In the sample to the right, I've used this form to suggest a garden of wildflowers. Depending on the colors and height, it can also represent leaves, shrubs, fireworks, feathers, fur or other fuzzy surface.

Visualize or mark an area that you wish to fill with this wildflower texture. You will be filling the area with tall stacks, each with a diamond-shaped top. To practice, use two colors of small seed beads, for example, green and pink.

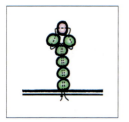

fig. 14
Make a diamond-shaped top on stack.

Sew to the surface, pick up four green beads and slide them along the thread to the surface of your fabric. The top of this stack will consist of three beads. Pick up one green bead, followed by one pink bead, then one green bead. Sew back through the holes of the four green beads closest to the fabric, and through the fabric to the wrong side. When you snug the thread tension, you will notice that the pink bead sits on top of the two green beads on either side of it, forming a diamond shape (fig. 14). Continue making diamond-topped stacks to fill the designated area.

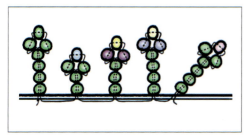

fig. 15
Here are a few possible variations.

In the sample above, I used four different colors (pink, light blue, medium blue and yellow) for the wildflowers. Many other variations are possible with this technique (fig. 15). Try using different colors of beads on either side of the point of the diamond to suggest a larger flower. Or use just one color of beads to represent shrubs with leaves. The stacks may be of any height and either straight or angled.

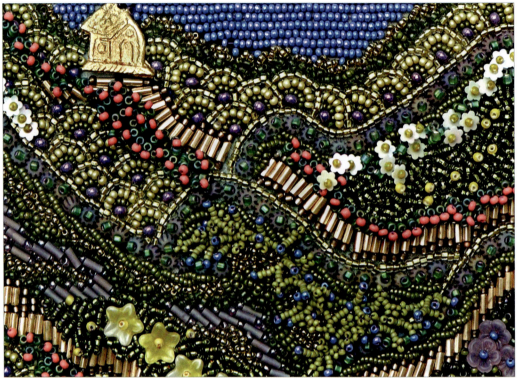

R. Atkins, 2000

Moss & Wildflowers

6" x 6.5", detail (See entire piece on page 29.)
Pink-tipped diamonds top tall stacks to suggest tiny wildflowers.

Rosie, The Uncaged Hen

6.5" x 5.5" x 2.5", sculpture, detail
Rosie is a three-dimensional chicken. I used the wildflower technique to cover her breast with texture and color.

R. Atkins, 2003

Running Water

Surface bumps may be crossed over and under each other to look like running water in a river or stream. By using shades of blue-green and a little white, bumps can be made to suggest waves or ripples on the surface of a stream, lake or the ocean.

To make a bump, bring the needle to the surface of the fabric and string three to five beads on the needle. Notice the length of these beads on your needle. Sew back down into the fabric less than this length away from where the bump starts (fig. 16). Depending on where you put the needle back into the fabric (the distance from the start of the bump), you can make the bump flat or raised (fig. 17).

Some of the bumps are only three beads long. Others are as many as nine beads long. I've positioned longer bumps so that they cross over the top of flatter or shorter bumps. You can also do it the other way around, making a longer, higher bump first and then a flatter bump under it.

In the sample above, I used all the same color of beads to suggest a river flowing from the mountains. See *Aqua* on page 35 as another example of this technique. Making overlapping bumps might also be used to create a dense, textured background or to suggest fields of grass.

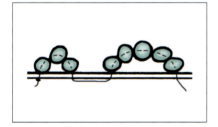

fig. 16
Bump center is above fabric surface.

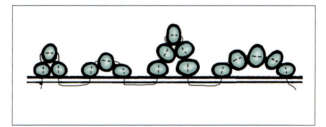

fig. 17
The spacing and height of bumps may be varied.

Petals

Surface bumps may be used to suggest small, three-dimensional flowers such as the ones in this sample. This technique also works well to create larger flowers with small, dense petals such as chrysanthemums.

To make small flowers like the three in the sample above, first make a center for the flower. This can be a single bead, a button or a seed bead circled by a ring of small seed beads (as in the sample above and fig. 18 below). Then sew a series of surface bumps around the center. To make a bump, bring the needle to the surface of the fabric next to the flower center, and string an odd number of beads (three, five or seven) on the needle. Sew back down into the fabric next to where the bump starts (fig. 19). Make another bump right next to the first one. Make bumps (petals) all around the center of the flower, spacing them evenly.

fig. 18
Make flower center.

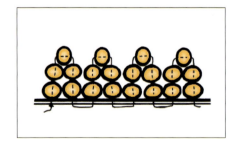

fig. 19
Make bumps as petals.

To make larger flowers, continue making bumps in concentric circles around the center of the flower. If you want the petals to stand out, change the color for each ring of petals. For example, the center of the flower could be a very pale yellow, and each ring of petals around it could be a slightly darker shade of yellow. The petals can all be the same size, or you can make longer petals on the outer rings by using more (or larger) beads for each bump.

Tree Trunks

By weaving or crossing surface bumps over and under each other, you can create a realistic-looking, three-dimensional tree trunk.

fig. 20
Cross the bumps.

First you may want to review the steps for making surface bumps on page 65. Next visualize or mark (page 10) the location of the desired tree trunk. Begin by making a few rather flat bumps at the base of the trunk. Make longer, taller bumps that cross over the tops of the first bumps, thus forming parallel, skinny X shapes (fig. 20). Fill in the lower portion of the trunk with more bumps. Continue adding crossing bumps in a vertical pattern to complete the trunk.

I Am A Tree

3.5" x 2.5", detail
This is a detail from the beaded cover of a hand-bound mini-book.

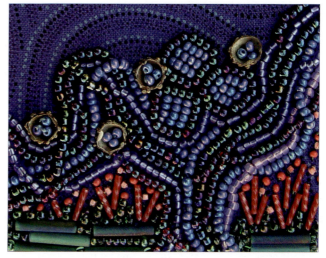

R. Atkins, 1996

Loops

Loopy surface fringe is an attractive textural addition to otherwise flat bead embroidery. I especially love to put a glass (or in the case of the sample to the left, mother-of-pearl) ring in each of the loops.

Sew to the surface of your beadwork in a place where you want a loop to originate. String one larger seed bead. String about 20 small seed beads. Sew back through the larger bead to the wrong side. Repeat these steps for more loops, if desired.

To make a loop with a ring in it (fig. 21), come to the surface, string one larger seed bead and string about 20 small seed beads. String the ring (making sure it slides easily over the small seed beads and sew back through the larger bead to the wrong side. The length of a loop can be adjusted by changing the number of small seed beads used to make it.

R. Atkins, 2003

Harvest

6.5" x 7.75", detail
This is a detail of beadwork inset in
the cover of a hand-bound book.

fig. 21
Put a ring through loop fringe.

Twisted Fringe

Twisted fringe on the surface of bead embroidery adds a textural element that suggests flowing motion. It can be used to represent hair, vines, seaweed, waterfalls, etc.

The keys to twisted fringe are using beads with very small holes and doubling your thread. I especially like Czech seed beads (size 12, 13 or 14) for twisted fringe.

Using a doubled thread, sew to the surface of your beadwork where you want the fringe to originate. String seed beads with extra small holes to a little more than double the desired length of the fringe. For example, if you want the fringe to be one inch long, string about two and a half inches of beads.

Lay your beadwork on the edge of a table and put some weight on it. (I use a four-pound diver's weight, but a box of beads or a bottle of water works fine.) Slide the beads toward your beadwork until they touch the fabric. Grab hold of the doubled thread just past the line of beads, and twist it in one direction between your thumb and first finger. Repeat the twisting motion several times.

While holding the doubled thread at the end of the line of beads, use your other hand to grab the center point in the line of beads. Bring the end of the line to meet the start of the line (at the fabric). Release your hold on the middle portion of the line. If you've twisted the thread enough, the fringe should twist by itself. Sometimes it needs a little coaxing.

If the fringe doesn't twist, even with a little coaxing, you will need to twist the doubled thread several more times. If repeated twists in the doubled thread do not make the fringe twist, then the holes of the beads are probably too large for the size of the thread you are using. Try a heavier thread or use beads with smaller holes.

Once the fringe twists properly, keep holding the doubled thread at the end of the line of beads and use your other hand to sew through the fabric next to the first bead of the fringe. Keep holding the doubled thread as you pull almost all of the extra length to the wrong side. At the last moment, release your grip and pull the doubled thread tight on the wrong side. Knot off on the wrong side after each twisted fringe.

R. Atkins, 2005

Mountains & Streams

left, 6" x 6.5", detail
The twisted lines on this piece give both definition and texture to the landscape. (See entire piece on page 31.)

Moss & Wildflowers

opposite page, 6" x 6.5", detail
(See entire piece on page 29.)

Twisted Lines

Twisted fringe can be sewn onto the beading surface with couching stitches to create a straight or curved textural, twisted line. I often use this technique when I want to emphasize a line. Also, it may be used to create an ornate border or frame.

First, review the directions for making twisted fringe (pages 69-70). Determine where you want to put the twisted line on the surface of your beadwork and how long it needs to be. Using double thread, sew to the surface of your beadwork at one end of the line. String seed beads with extra small holes. You will need double the length of the line, plus about 10 percent extra. Twist the fringe and check the length. If the twisted fringe is too long or too short, you will need to adjust the number of beads and re-twist. Sew through the fabric and knot off on the wrong side when it looks right.

Use couching stitches (page 61) to attach the fringe to the beading surface. Snip one of the threads about a half inch from the knot on the wrong side. Using the remaining single thread, sew to the surface next to the first twist, where the two strands cross. Sew over the lower strand (between two beads) and through the fabric to the wrong side. Sew to the surface next to the second twist. Sew over the lower strand (between two beads) and through the fabric to the wrong side. Repeat, until all points where the strands cross are couched (secured) to the fabric. At the end of the twisted line of beads, there will be a small loop. Sew to the surface inside and at the end of the loop. Then sew over the end of the loop (between two beads) and through the fabric to the wrong side. Knot off on the wrong side.

R. Atkins, 2000

Smoke

Twisted fringe, attached to the fabric with couching stitches, may be used to suggest smoke or steam. Do you see a volcano blowing steam in the sample to the left?

First, you may wish to review the directions for making twisted fringe (pages 69-70). Determine how long the plume of smoke or steam needs to be. Using double thread, sew to the surface of your bead work where the plume will originate. String seed beads with extra small holes. You will need double the length of the plume, plus about 10 percent extra. Twist the fringe, hold in place and check the length. If the twisted fringe is too long or too short, adjust the number of beads and re-twist. Sew through the fabric and knot off on the wrong side when it looks right.

Use couching stitches to attach the fringe to the beading surface (page 61 and 71). Knot off on the wrong side. Repeat the steps above to make additional smoke plumes.

Decade Doll #4

5" x 4.5", detail
(See complete doll on page 11.)

R. Atkins, 2007

Branch Fringe

Branch fringe (also known as "kinky fringe") may be couched onto the surface of your bead embroidery to add fuzzy texture. I also use it to suggest shrubs, fields of grass or strands of kelp in the water.

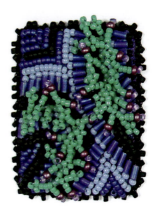

It works really well to leave a small area of your bead embroidery unbeaded, and then fill the area with branch fringe. You can also make a line of branch fringe and couch it down next to an existing line of beads, as I've done in the sample above. I tend to use either size 15 or size 11 seed beads for branch fringe. If you are making a line of branch fringe, measure the length of the line and make the fringe that long. If you are filling an area with branch fringe, make the fringe about three times as long as the diameter of the area.

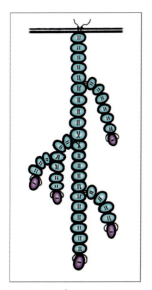

fig. 22
Make branch fringe.

To make branch fringe, sew to the surface of your beading surface at the point where you want the fringe to start. String beads to the pre-determined length of the fringe. Skipping the last bead, sew back through a few of the strung beads (the stem of the fringe). Snug the fringe tight and string on a few beads for the first branch. Skipping the last bead of the branch, sew back through the branch and up the stem a short distance. Snug the fringe tight and string on a few beads for the second branch. Work your way up the stem, adding branches every few beads (fig. 22). Note that you can make a very full fringe by adding twigs to the branches (see middle branch in drawing to the left). After making the final branch, sew through the remaining beads of the stem and through the fabric to the wrong side, and knot.

If you are making a line of branch fringe, position the fringe along the line and couch it in place using the following method.

Sew to the surface next to the fringe about one half inch from the start of the fringe. Sew over the stem of the fringe (so that the thread rests between two beads) and through the fabric to the wrong side. Sew to the surface again about one half inch further down the length of the fringe. Sew over the stem of the fringe and through the fabric to the wrong side. Continue couching the fringe to the fabric about every half inch to the end of the fringe (page 61). I generally do not couch the branches to the fabric unless they are quite long or I want to position them a certain way.

If you are filling an unbeaded area with fringe, "scramble" the whole fringe into the area and hold in place loosely. Couch it in place using the following method. Sew to the surface anywhere within the area and sew over the nearest part of the fringe (so that the thread rests between two beads) and through the fabric to the wrong side. Sew to the surface again one fourth to one half inch away, and sew over the nearest part of the fringe. Continue to make random couching stitches until the fringe is secured in the area.

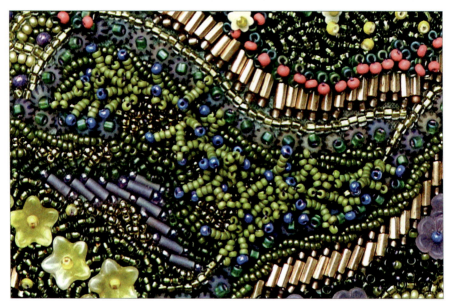

R. Atkins, 2000

Moss & Wildflowers

6" x 6.5", detail (See entire piece on page 29.)
A long branch fringe is "scrambled" and couched down, filling an irregular area.

Tree Branches

Branch fringe lives up to its name with this technique. By stitching a diamond ending at the tip of each branch, you can create a realistic representation of real branches and leaves. By adding a few small flower beads, you can suggest springtime and ornamental fruit trees!

Making branches and leaves combines three techniques previously described: branch fringe (pages 73-74), tree trunks (page 67) and the diamond-shaped ending used to suggest wildflowers (page 63). I generally use size 11 or size 15 beads for this technique.

fig. 23

Start by making overlapping bumps to form the tree trunk. When the trunk is complete, create a length of branch fringe, originating in an appropriate place and using the same color beads as the trunk. For each twig off the main branch (or stem) of the fringe, string several tree-color beads followed by four green beads. Skipping the last three of the green beads, sew back through the first green bead and the tree-colored beads to create a twig with a green, diamond-shaped tip (fig. 23), representing a leaf.

Continue adding twigs to the main branch, working your way back to the start of the fringe. Position the fringe on your fabric and couch it down (page 61) every one fourth to one half inch. I generally do not couch down the twigs, as I like dimensionality and movement. Sometimes it helps to control the direction a twig points by couching it down after the first or second bead (closest to the main stem of the fringe).

Make additional fringes to represent other branches on your tree. Generally, I add the background beads after I have completed the tree, as in the sample above. However, it also works to sew a solid background of beads first and then make the branches, couching them on top of the background beads for added dimension and texture.

R. Atkins, 2007

Respect

6" x 4", detail
Bead Journal Project, October
(See entire piece on page 17.)

Roots

Branch fringe makes fabulous roots! Use this technique to represent realistic root systems, as seen in a cross-sectional view of the earth. Also, use it symbolically to represent the "rooted" or "grounded" nature of a person in an abstract beaded portrait.

Generally, I begin by beading the surface line of the earth. Next, I add some underground "rocks," using small accent beads, such as stone or bone "chips." I use size 15 or size 11 seed beads for the root system. To make branch fringe (which will become the root system), I start at the surface line.

Determine the approximate length of the root system and string that length of seed beads for the stem of the fringe. Skipping the last bead, sew back through a few of the strung beads. Snug the fringe tight and string on a few beads for the first branch. Skipping the last bead of the branch, sew back through the branch and up the stem a short distance. Snug the fringe tight and string on a few beads for the second branch. Repeat, adding branches and working your way back to the starting point of the fringe. I tend to make long branches with several shorter branches off of each one (page 73, fig. 22, middle branch).

Position the fringe on your fabric, draping the branches around the bead "rocks." Couch it down (page 61) every one fourth to one half inch. I generally do not couch the small branch roots down, as I like dimensionality and movement.

You may want to make more than one fringe to represent the entire root system in your design, such as for a large tree (for example, see *Madrona*, page 34). You can allow the fabric to show as the background behind the roots (for example, see *Self Portrait*, page 22 and *Mom's Pouch*, page 27). Or, if you prefer, you can sew a solid background of beads, as in the sample above. You can add the background beads after couching your root system in place, or you can bead the background first and then couch the roots on top of it.

A few closing thoughts

My earliest ideas and notes for this book go back nearly four years, when I was first starting to make the series of Decade Dolls on the cover. Working on the dolls was a fascinating and self-actualizing process, one that made me feel more confident as an artist, certainly, and more accepting of myself as a person. While making the last of the dolls (see page 3), representing my life story from ages 51 through 60, I found myself thinking about how much I wanted to share the gift of this idea with others.

At the same time, while teaching bead embroidery, I realized I'd outgrown the two-day class. I could no longer teach all the fabulous techniques and variations I know in two days. The answer, obviously, was to write another book, a companion to my first book, *One Bead at a Time*. All excited about the idea, I immediately noted on my website that the new book would be out sometime in 2006.

It's a good thing it took longer than expected because, in the meantime, I've discovered more ideas and new techniques. More importantly, the 2007 Bead Journal Project began and was the inspiration for visual journaling with beads. As of this writing, I have completed nine pieces for the Bead Journal Project, eight of which are included in this book.

Although I've been making my living with beads for over 20 years, my passion for beads and thirst for knowledge about them is as strong as it was at the beginning. Of all the ways I've learned to work with beads (weaving, stringing, wire working and embellishing), bead embroidery continues to delight and challenge me more than anything else. As long as my eyes and dexterity hold out, I'll be sewing beads on fabric for many more years to come.

It is my fondest hope that you'll find inspiration and ideas here to give you similar pleasure and satisfaction with bead embroidery. May your creativity and confidence as an artist flourish with every bead you stitch. May your heart speak through your hands and beads, bringing greater joy, harmony and acceptance into your life. Beady blessings!

Robin Atkins

Other books by Robin Atkins

One Bead at a Time, Exploring Creativity with Bead Embroidery, ISBN: 0-9705538-2-X, c. 2000. Learn to sew beads on fabric improvisationally using basic stitches and variations. Explore the creative process and see how beads, creativity, healing and art are related.

Beaded Embellishment, Techniques & Designs for Embroidering on Cloth, co-author, Amy Clarke, ISBN: 1-931499-12-8, c. 2002. This definitive book about bead embroidery includes techniques, design ideas, ten lovely projects and a gallery.

Spirit Dolls, ISBN: 0-9705538-4-6, c. 2005. Learn to make cloth spirit dolls and embellish them with beads and fringe. This book includes patterns, instructions and tips to design your own unique and personal dolls.

Beaded Treasures, Finger Woven Bracelets, Necklaces, Tassels & Straps, ISBN: 978-0-9-705538-6-7, c. 2006. Step-by-step instructions for designing and weaving original beaded jewelry to showcase your favorite beads.

Robin has also written *Finishing Techniques for Bead Embroidery Projects, How I Made Rosie, The Uncaged Hen* and the text for a photography book, *Nautical Highways, Ferries of the San Juan Islands.*

All of Robin's books are available to order through her website, where you will also find a gallery of her beadwork, technical and artistic tips, a link to *Beadlust* (her blog) and more.

www.robinatkins.com

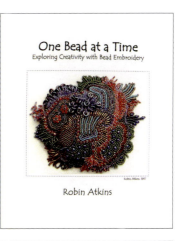

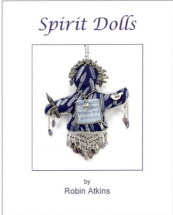

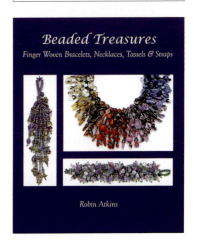

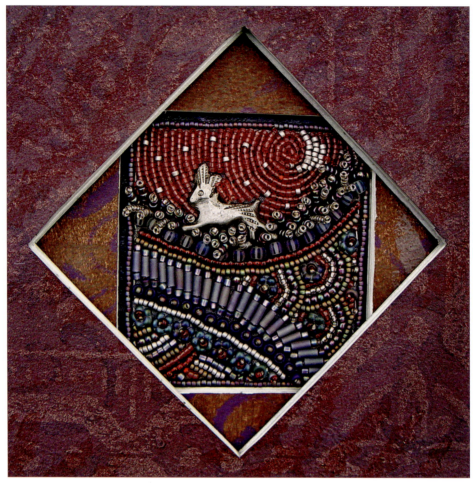

R. Atkins, 2004

Thank you!

Thank you for joining me on this journey
toward creating art with beads!